THE
LIFE
of
SAINT
NICHOLAS

As Transcribed

in Pictures

and Text

By

R. O. Blechman

TEXT AND ILLUSTRATIONS COPYRIGHT © 1996 R.O. BLECHMAN

PUBLISHED IN 1996 AND DISTRIBUTED IN THE U.S. BY
STEWART, TABORI & CHANG,
A DIVISION OF U.S. MEDIA HOLDINGS, INC.
575 BROADWAY, NEW YORK, N.Y. 10012

DISTRIBUTED IN CANADA BY
GENERAL PUBLISHING CO. LTD.
30 LESMILL ROAD
DON MILLS, ONTARIO, CANADA M3B 2T6

DISTRIBUTED IN AUSTRALIA AND NEW ZEALAND BY
PERIBO PTY LTD.
58 BEAUMONT ROAD, MOUNT KURING-GAI
NSW 2080, AUSTRALIA

DISTRIBUTED IN ALL OTHER TERRITORIES BY
GRANTHAM BOOK SERVICES LTD.
ISAAC NEWTON WAY, ALMA PARK INDUSTRIAL ESTATE
GRANTHAM, LINCOLNSHIRE NG31 9SD, ENGLAND

LIBRARY OF CONGRESS CATALOG CARD NUMBER: 96-686 16

ISBN: 1-55670-506-9

PRINTED IN SINGAPORE
10 9 8 7 6 5 4 3 2 1

TO
NICHOLAS
&
MAX

LITTLE WAS KNOWN
OF SAINT NICHOLAS'S
ACTUAL LIFE
UNTIL THE DISCOVERY
IN 1989
OF AN ANCIENT MANSCRIPT

("VITA SPLENDIDA ET ILLUSTRIS
DE NICOLO BEATO")

THE DISCOVERY WAS MADE BY AN
ITALIAN FARMER DIGGING FOR
TRUFFLES.

Piano!
Piano!

THE MANUSCRIPT WAS BROUGHT
TO THE ATTENTION OF THE LOCAL
PRIEST, FATHER BENEDETTI.

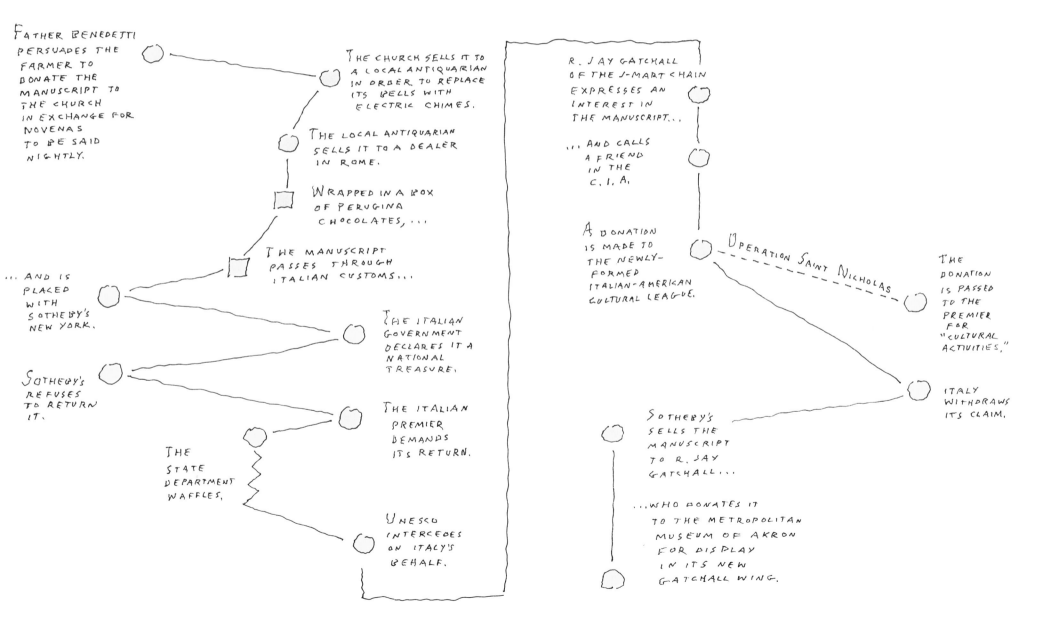

HERE IT BEGAN ITS TRAVELS TO ITS FINAL DESTINATION.

FATHER BENEDETTI PERSUADES THE FARMER TO DONATE THE MANUSCRIPT TO THE CHURCH IN EXCHANGE FOR NOVENAS TO BE SAID NIGHTLY.

THE CHURCH SELLS IT TO A LOCAL ANTIQUARIAN IN ORDER TO REPLACE ITS BELLS WITH ELECTRIC CHIMES.

THE LOCAL ANTIQUARIAN SELLS IT TO A DEALER IN ROME.

WRAPPED IN A BOX OF PERUGINA CHOCOLATES, ...

THE MANUSCRIPT PASSES THROUGH ITALIAN CUSTOMS...

... AND IS PLACED WITH SOTHEBY'S NEW YORK.

THE ITALIAN GOVERNMENT DECLARES IT A NATIONAL TREASURE.

SOTHEBY'S REFUSES TO RETURN IT.

THE ITALIAN PREMIER DEMANDS ITS RETURN.

THE STATE DEPARTMENT WAFFLES,

UNESCO INTERCEDES ON ITALY'S BEHALF.

R. JAY GATCHALL OF THE J-MART CHAIN EXPRESSES AN INTEREST IN THE MANUSCRIPT...

... AND CALLS A FRIEND IN THE C.I.A.

A DONATION IS MADE TO THE NEWLY-FORMED ITALIAN-AMERICAN CULTURAL LEAGUE.

OPERATION SAINT NICHOLAS

THE DONATION IS PASSED TO THE PREMIER FOR "CULTURAL ACTIVITIES,"

ITALY WITHDRAWS ITS CLAIM.

SOTHEBY'S SELLS THE MANUSCRIPT TO R. JAY GATCHALL...

...WHO DONATES IT TO THE METROPOLITAN MUSEUM OF AKRON FOR DISPLAY IN ITS NEW GATCHALL WING.

Housed in Akron,
the manuscript sheds
important light
on the life of the legendary
Saint Nicholas.

THE LI

SAINT

"VITA SPLENDIDA et I

E OF

ICHOLAS

STRIS DE NICOLO BEATO"

THE FATHER OF SAINT NICHOLAS,
POMPUS PLUVIUS, WAS A WEALTHY
MANUFACTURER OF GREEK STATUES.

APHRODITE

NIKE

POMPUS PLUVIUS

DISCOBOLUS

LAOCOÖN

HIS BUSINESS SUFFERED DURING THE
REIGN OF EMPEROR CONSTANTINE (A.D. 274-337)
WHEN CHRISTIANITY BECAME THE
STATE RELIGION (A.D. 313).

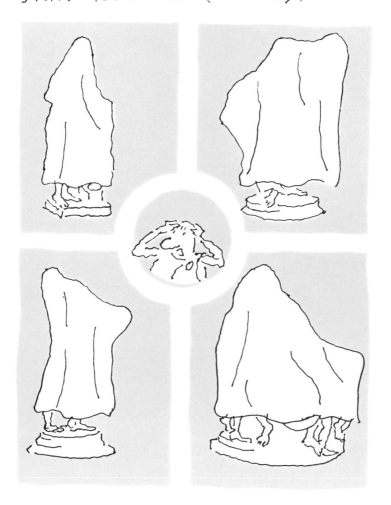

However he quickly adapted
to the new religion.

THE MADONNA

THE ANNUNCIATION

JESUS CASTING OUT
THE MONEY CHANGERS

THE THREE MAGI

IN A.D. 314 HIS WIFE BORE HIM
AN ONLY SON, NICHOLAS,

THE CHILD DEMONSTRATED EXTRAORDINARY POWERS AT AN EARLY AGE.

It must be the spoon. Soft metal.
We'll get him a silver spoon.
Eat from the silver spoon, darling!
Look! Your bowl is silver, too!
I think we've got a problem!

AT FIRST, NICHOLAS PERFORMED TRICKS
FOR HIS OWN AMUSEMENT, ...

BENDING KNIVES, ...

TWISTING HALOS, ...

... FILLING WINE BOWLS WITH VINEGAR, ...

... AND VINEGAR JARS WITH WINE.

BUT IN A.D. 326, WHEN HE TURNED TWELVE,
HIS LIFE UNDERWENT A CHANGE,

They look so wretched!
snap!

Of course they do. They're poor. Now close the curtain, dear.
But why?
Because the light hurts your father and he needs the rest.
But why are all these people poor?
The poor are with us always, dear. Even the Bible says so. Now close the curtain. Your father had a hard day at the foundry.

NICHOLAS RETURNED THE NEXT DAY.

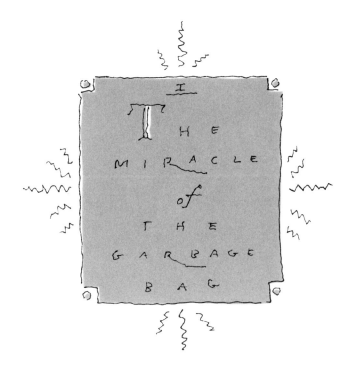

I

THE
MIRACLE
of
THE
GARBAGE
BAG

Make it quick, before the garbage collector comes!
Yes, father.

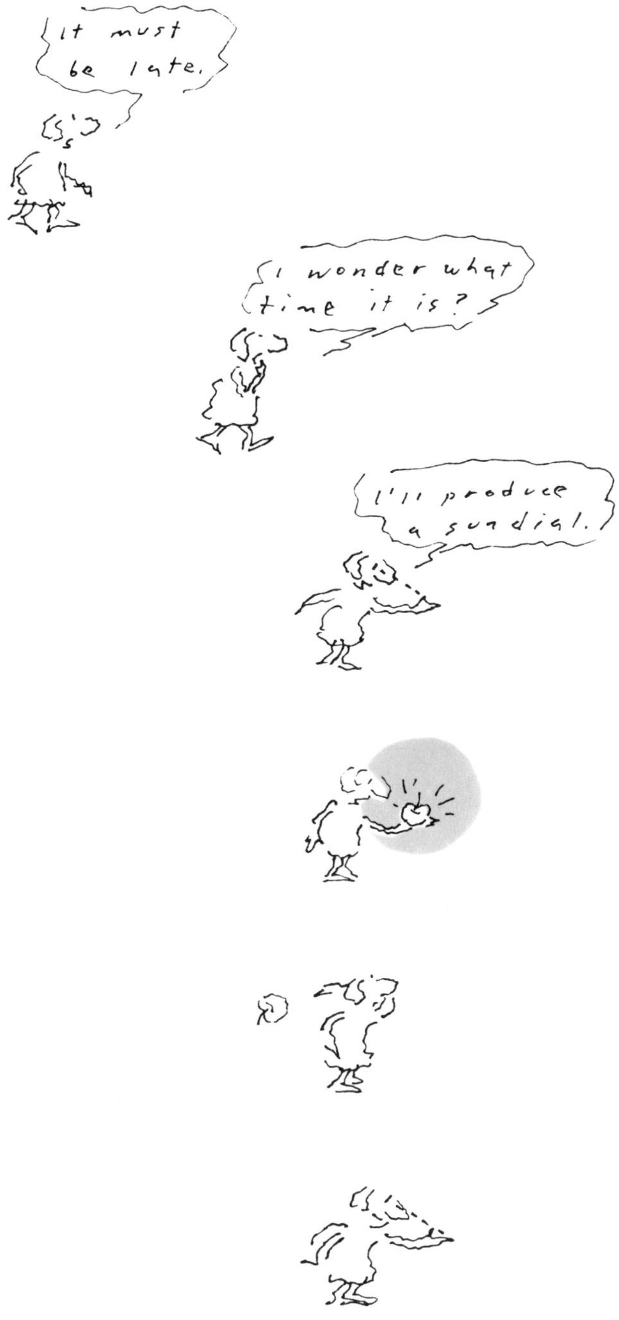
It must be late.
I wonder what time it is?
I'll produce a sundial.

well, one miracle
a day is enough!

THE WINTER OF A.D. 330, WHEN NICHOLAS TURNED SIXTEEN, WAS SEVERE.

IT WAS IN A SNOWSTORM THAT NICHOLAS PERFORMED HIS NEXT MIRACLE.

scratch

scratch

scratch

II

THE MIRACLE
of
THE
FUR-LINED
COAT

CONCERNED BY HIS FAILURE TO PERFORM MORE MIRACLES, NICHOLAS SPOKE TO HIS CLOSE FRIEND, CRITIUS.

Look, I'm a writer.
I go through periods
when I can't write,
So what do I do?

I forget about
writing.
I go to the beach...
I swim....
I drink in the sun...
And then, when
I least expect it...
KNOCK, KNOCK!
Who's there?
I open the door
And there she is....
...

My Muse!
And I start
writing again!

ONE EVENING, AS NICHOLAS PASSED
BELOW THE WINDOW OF A SEASIDE VILLA,
HE OVERHEARD A STRANGE CONVERSATION.

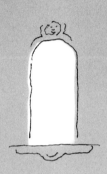

THE
MIRACLE
of
THE
THREE
VIRGINS

Don't cry, mother, father. All is not lost. There is something to sell.
Go back to bed, Virgilia. There's nothing you can do!
But there is something to sell.
PRUDENTIA! CARITA!

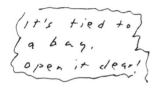

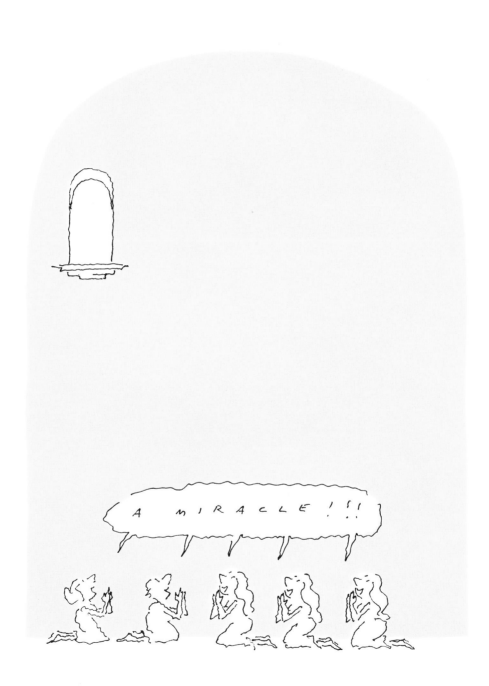

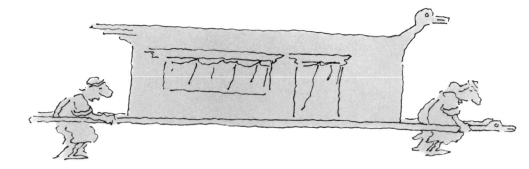

why are they here?
while you were away, dear, the Emperor died— your color is so much better!— and our new Emperor is a pagan.
So no miracles, please, son!
Listen to your father, we're pagans now.
We're Pagans, and I don't want you to forget it.
So be a good boy— put your cloak on rightside out!— and we'll talk in the morning.

NICHOLAS WANDERED THE ROMAN EMPIRE
FOR THE NEXT FEW YEARS.

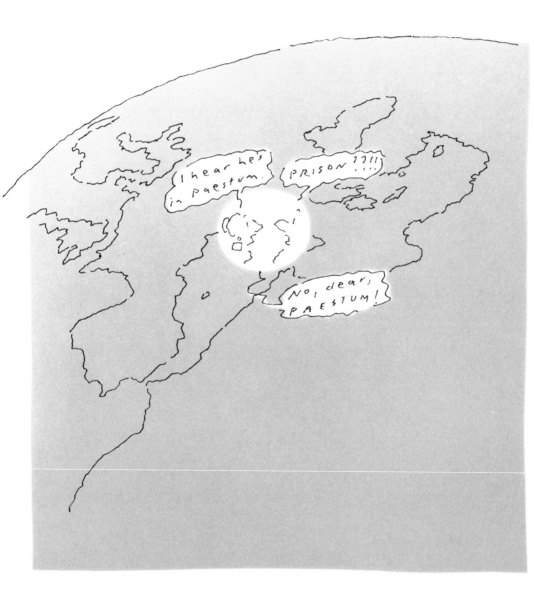

HIS PARENTS GREW OLD.

IN A.D. 362 HE WAS ARRESTED IN PALMYRA.

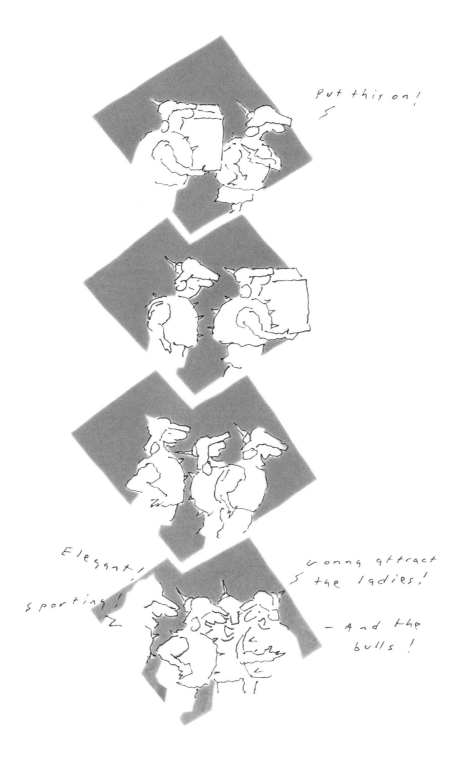

A dunce cap!

He likes to
give things
away....

so he needs...

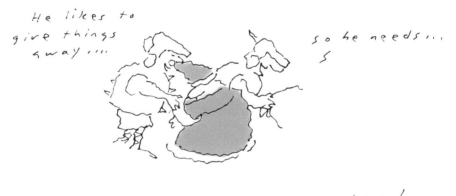

...a bag!

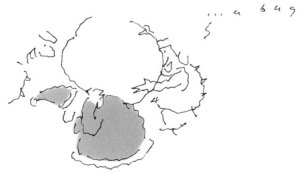

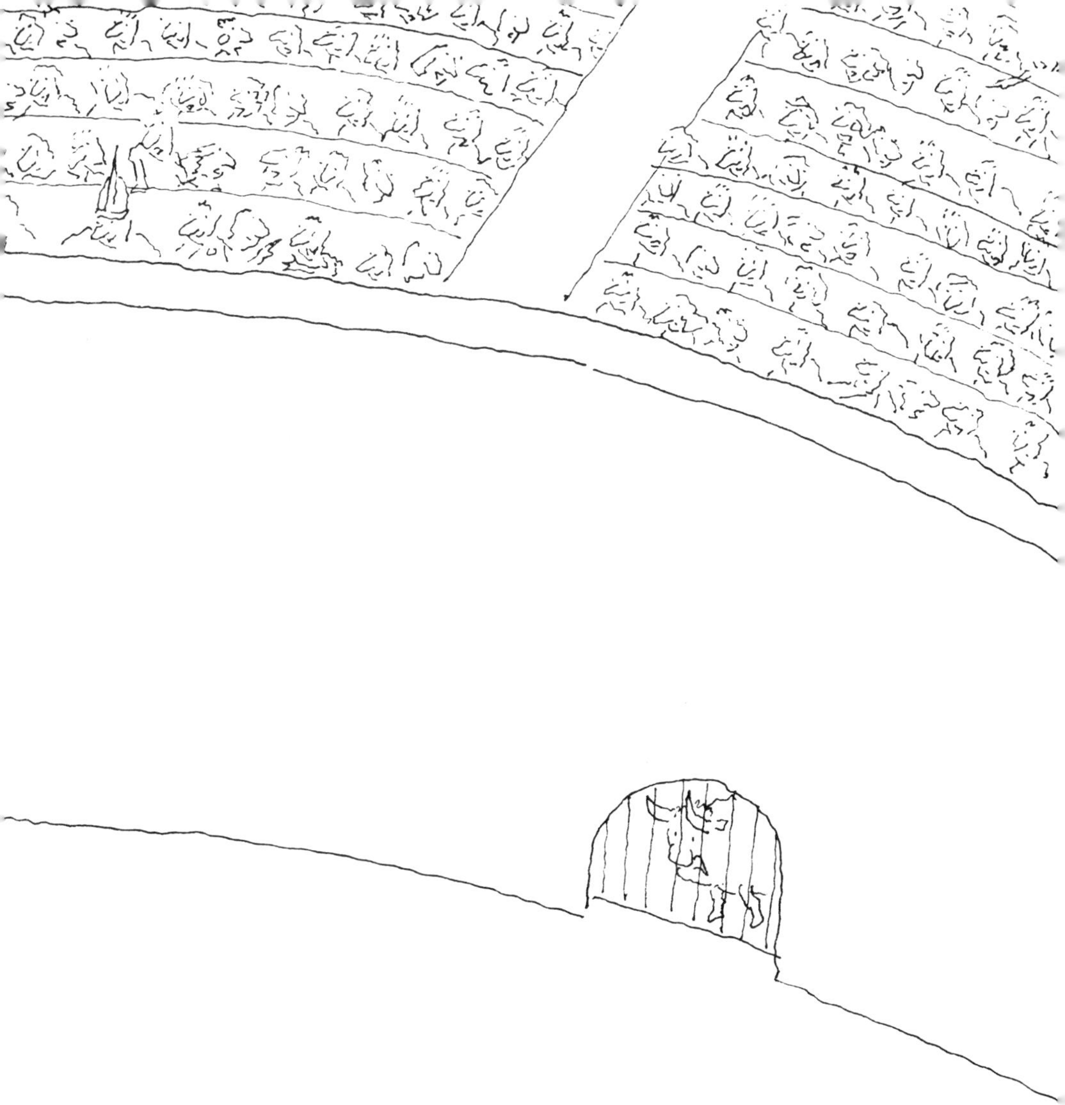

HERE THE
KNOWN FACTS
of
SAINT NICHOLAS'S
LIFE END.
——o——

THE FINAL LEAVES OF THE MANUSCRIPT WERE LOST TO HISTORY

PORCA MISERIA!
CHE FAI?!

Cretino!

According to
Legend
Saint Nicholas
Performed
a final
Miracle.

IV

THE
MIRACLE
of
THE
AMPITHEATRE

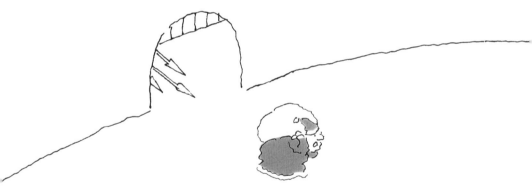

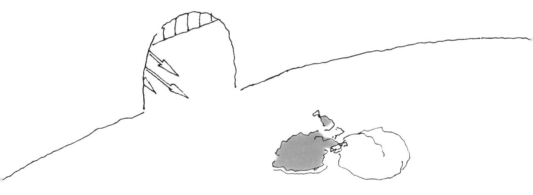

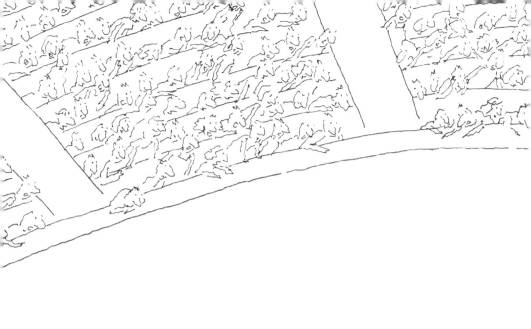

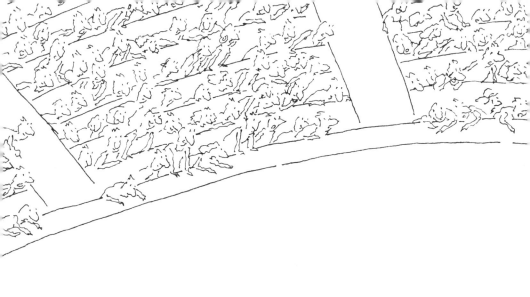

THE
END

SPECIAL OFFER
TO
OUR READERS

▷

YOU CAN OWN AN AUTHENTIC
SAINT NICHOLAS T-SHIRT
AUTHORIZED BY J-MART
& THE METROPOLITAN MUSEUM OF AKRON!

– – – – – – – – – – – – – PLEASE PHOTOCOPY AND SEND – – – – – – – – – – –
ENCLOSED IS MY CHECK FOR ONLY $12.95
(POSTAGE AND HANDLING INCLUDED)

LAST NAME _____ FIRST NAME _____

STREET ADDRESS _____

CITY _____ STATE _____ ZIP CODE _____

(SEND COUPON & PAYMENT TO: SAINT NICHOLAS,
BOX 998, KNICKERBOCKER STATION,
NEW YORK, N.Y. 10002)